Saying It Like It Is

Some of the photographs in this book have special significance to the author. For details, see pages 155-56.

Saying It Like It Is

SHERI DEW

DESERET
BOOK

SALT LAKE CITY, UTAH

Library of Congress Cataloging-in-Publication Data

Dew, Sheri L.
 Saying it like it is / Sheri Dew.
   p. cm.
 ISBN 978-1-60641-087-5 (hardbound : alk. paper)
 1. Christian life—Mormon authors. 2. Christianity. I. Title.
 BX8656.D49 2009
 248.4088'2893—dc22

                                    2008043004

Printed in Mexico
R. R. Donnelley and Sons, Reynosa, Mexico
10   9   8   7   6   5   4   3   2   1

*N*oble and great. Courageous and determined.
Faithful and fearless. That is who you are and who
you have always been. And understanding it can
change your life, because this knowledge carries a
confidence that cannot be duplicated any other way.

It is actually easier to motivate someone

to do something difficult than something easy.

That's because the status quo is uninspiring.

Our spirits crave to progress, and if we aren't

moving forward, we're not happy.

2

4

We may not be the first generation of sisters to be influenced by the world, but we need to be the last. We've just got to be the last. It is high time for us to arise and have the influence God intended us to have. It is high time for us to lead the women of the world. It is high time for us to model the distinctiveness and happiness that set true followers of Jesus Christ apart.

*T*hose who think of life as a personal ministry tend to be less lonely, less likely to feel that life has spun out of control, more inclined to have a gentle heart, more filled with purpose.

Holiness means walking away from the philosophies of man.

It means looking to prophets for spiritual counsel, not celebrities or

experts, who may be appealing but who all come packing personal

motives and an arsenal of half-truths. It is deadly to take counsel from

anyone whose primary motive is to build his or her own kingdom.

There are some who make living the gospel seem like a sentence to life on the rock pile. It's not living the gospel that's hard. It's life that's hard. It's picking up the pieces when covenants have been compromised or values violated that's hard. The gospel is the Good News that provides us the tools to cope with the mistakes, the heartaches, the disappointments we can expect to experience here.

The doctrine of the Atonement is a
doctrine of healing. The Savior heals us from
the effects of sin, when we repent. He heals our
weaknesses and mistakes. He heals broken
promises, broken lives, broken hearts. When we
demonstrate the faith to seek after Him, and try
our best to follow Him, He will heal us.

*B*eing steadfast and immovable on the Lord's side of the line is the only strategy that works long-term against Lucifer. If the adversary can't get us to succumb to blatant evil, he tries to wear us down, weaken our resolve, and dim our memory of who we are. He promotes the Sin Now, Pay Later Plan. He feeds our vanity with promises of popularity and power. He tells us that life is supposed to be easy and that if we experience undeserved pain the gospel must not be true. He always promises shortcuts, though there are no shortcuts to anywhere worth going. But he cannot duplicate joy or peace. That is why there is such safety on the Lord's side of the line, where the power of the priesthood and the Holy Ghost protect us.

The Holy Ghost is always the

Teacher anytime, anywhere pure

truth is taught. That is His privilege;

that is His stewardship.

The gift of the Holy Ghost is a gift of power. The Holy Ghost inspires and heals, guides and warns, enhances our natural capacities, inspires charity and humility, makes us smarter than we are, strengthens us during trials, testifies of the Father and the Son, and shows us "all things" that we should do. He helps us do more and become more than we could ever do or become on our own.

A half-hearted effort to keep the Sabbath Day holy or to be morally clean is really no effort at all. Eight percent of your increase isn't tithing, it's a donation. The Lord didn't declare, "Thou shalt not steal—unless you're in a real bind." He said, "Thou shalt not," clearly delineating the lines we are not to cross—lines that represent breaches in integrity or morality or virtue so serious that they drive the Spirit away and lead ultimately to the destruction of our souls.

Living as Latter-day Saints is not easy. But it is easier than the alternative. The cost of discipleship, as high as it may be, is less than the price of sin—less costly than having the Holy Ghost withdraw or losing self-respect or jeopardizing eternal life.

*C*hallenges that tax our faith are usually opportunities to stretch and strengthen our faith by finding out if we really believe the Lord will help us.

The compelling truth of the Restoration is that the heavens are open. This Church is a Church of revelation. Our challenge is not one of getting the Lord to speak to us. Our challenge is learning to hear what He has to say.

*T*rue leaders understand that leadership

is not about them but about those they

serve. It is not about exalting themselves

but about lifting others up.

Coming unto Christ means walking away from the world. And walking away from the world means choosing holiness and purity over worldliness and impurity. Our Father wants us back, and He wants us back clean.

As daughters of our Heavenly Father, and as daughters of Eve, we are all mothers and we have always been mothers. And we each have the responsibility and the privilege to love and to help lead the rising generation. How will our young women learn to live as women of God unless they see what women of God look like— meaning what we wear, watch, and read; how we fill our time and our minds; how we face temptation and uncertainty; where we find true joy; and why modesty and femininity are hallmarks of righteous women? It is our responsibility to pass along the legacy of what it means to be a woman of God to the next generation.

We are here on earth now because we were

chosen to be here now. Our foreordination, however,

is not a guarantee. It is an indication of profound,

divine confidence. But it is not a guarantee.

Immersion in the word of God changes us.

It transforms those who plumb its depths.

It changes those who are just beginning to taste

the sweetness of the goodness of God.

When we really believe in Jesus Christ—meaning that He knows who we are and will overrule for our good—that kind of faith naturally results in a feeling of hope and optimism. We can hope not just for a better world somewhere out in the great beyond, but for a better world here and now.

*I*n today's world, there are too many good people

with no conviction, and too many evil people filled

with conviction. The world is crying out for leader-

ship—which is why these are the days in which a true

leader wants to live, for the opportunities to change

lives and even destinies are endless.

On those days when we're not ready to stop being offended, not ready to forgive, still determined to dish out the silent treatment, what we're actually saying is, "Thanks, but I don't want to become more like the Savior today. Maybe tomorrow, but not today." Perhaps those are the times when we need to pray the hardest, the times it becomes clear that a change in behavior is not enough —that we must have a change in nature.

There is nothing more vital to our success and our happiness here than learning to hear the voice of the Spirit. It is the Spirit who reveals to us our identity, which isn't just who we are but who we have always been. And when we know that, our lives take on a sense of purpose so compelling that we can never be the same again.

If we will learn to draw upon the power of God, we will not shrink. We will go forward, unflinching, unswerving, indomitable, making the world safer and cleaner, until we've done everything we were born to do. For we were born to lead. We were born to build Zion. We were born for glory. Everything we do in life should be measured against this grand standard.

We dare listen to the world only with our spiritual ears.

Beware of those who profess Christ while spewing subtle anti-Christ

statements. Anyone who professes to believe in Jesus Christ but denies

His divinity, no matter how many good deeds that person has done,

is anti-Christ. Anyone who shifts our focus away from making and

keeping covenants is a servant of Satan. Anything that keeps us out

of the temple or threatens the family is the work of Satan.

The fruits of priesthood power are for everyone. Uncategorically. Undeniably. And without restriction to those who qualify. One reason some may feel unsettled in their feelings about the priesthood is that we sometimes confuse the privilege of holding the priesthood with the blessings of the priesthood.

We are here to influence the world

rather than to be influenced by the world.

If we could unleash the full influence of

covenant-keeping women, the kingdom

of God would change overnight.

49

Do we know what we believe? Do we know there is power in the doctrine of Christ to change and overcome weakness? Do we realize that the scriptures contain the answer to every life dilemma? Do we know enough about our doctrine to discern the artful packaging of transgression so blatant in the world today? A casual understanding of the gospel will not sustain us through the days ahead, which is why it is imperative that we immerse ourselves in the word of God.

The only way to be happy is to live the gospel. It is not possible to sin enough to be happy. It isn't possible to buy enough to be happy, or to entertain or indulge or pamper ourselves enough to be happy. Happiness and joy come only when we are living up to who we are.

While we tend to equate motherhood solely with maternity, in the Lord's language, the word *mother* has layers of meaning. Of all the words they could have chosen to define her role and her essence, both God the Father and Adam called Eve "the mother of all living," and they did so before she ever bore a child. Like Eve, our motherhood began before we were born. Motherhood is more than bearing children, though it is certainly that. It is the essence of who we are as women.

$\mathcal{E}$very relationship—husband and wife, parent

and child, best friends, colleagues—is dependent on

trust. It is not possible to have a relationship with

someone you cannot trust. The only thing you can

have with someone you can't trust is a strategy.

It is simply not for us to judge each

other. The Lord has reserved that right for

Himself, because only He knows our hearts

and understands the varying circumstances

and complexities of our lives.

In this great latter-day battle, the Lord needs every true follower to step forward—in every part of His kingdom—to draw upon and use every gift and endowment we've been given. There isn't a week, a day, an hour to lose.

Every time we build the faith or reinforce the nobility of a young woman or man, every time we love or lead anyone even one small step along the path, we are true to our endowment and calling and inherent nature as mothers. No woman who understands the gospel would ever think that any other work is more important or would ever say, "I am just a mother," for mothers heal the souls of men.

When women understand and fully respect the fact

that the Church is governed by the power of the priesthood,

and when priesthood leaders acknowledge the unique and

vital contribution of women, the work can move forward

to bless the kingdom of God.

No amount of time in front of the

mirror will make us as attractive as does

having the Holy Ghost with us.

You ou are here now because you were divinely elected to be

here now. The simple fact and plain truth is that Mary and Eve

and countless other glorious women as well as countless spiritually

resplendent men were not assigned to this dispensation. We were.

*S*piritual privileges that call forth the powers of heaven are available to all who diligently seek them. The question, then, is, Will we diligently seek? In a classic address, Alma taught: "Whosoever will come may come and partake of the waters of life freely; and whosoever will not come the same is not compelled to come" (Alma 42:27). Alma didn't say that just the popular ones or the smart ones on full scholarship or the ones who got married at twenty-one may come. He said whosoever will—meaning, it is our choice.

The truth is that rarely does anything of the world—a new possession, a new toy, a new anything—result in joy. Joy is carried into the hearts of men and women by the Holy Ghost, who is unimpressed by bank accounts, titles, or products that roll off the assembly line. It is quite possible to be happy without owning much of this world's goods. It is not possible, however, to be truly happy without the abiding, sustaining presence of the Holy Ghost.

It takes the elect to gather the elect. That is who we are. And no one can take our place in doing it—whether it be our place in our families, or among our colleagues and friends, or in the world at large. No one, absolutely no one, can do what we have been sent here to do.

*B*urdens have the potential to exalt us, but baggage just weighs us down and wears us out. When we don't repent, sin becomes baggage. Worry, jealousy, and guilt are baggage. An unforgiving heart, anger, regret, and pride are baggage. We choose whether or not to pick up baggage, and Satan loves nothing more than loading us down like pack mules.

Why have prophets taught the doctrine of motherhood—and it is doctrine—from the beginning of time? Because we must be clear about the issues that swirl around our gender. For Satan has declared war on motherhood. He knows that those who rock the cradle can rock his earthly empire. And he knows that without righteous mothers loving and leading the next generation, the kingdom of God will fail.

The gift of charity is the greatest of all the gifts of the Spirit. But it may be the most underestimated. We tend to define charity as something we do or feel. But in our Father's vernacular, charity means much more. It is the word He uses to describe the character, nature, and very essence of His Son. Charity is who the Savior is. So when we plead for the gift of charity, we aren't asking for lovely feelings towards someone who bugs us or has injured us. We are actually pleading for our natures to be changed and for our character to become more and more like the Savior's.

No finer group of women have ever walked this earth. That is doctrine. You are here now because our Father chose you to be here now. That is doctrine. There is no way to limit the influence of a woman who is a true follower of Jesus Christ—a woman who devotes her energy to becoming more and more like Him. A woman who wants His nature to become her nature. That is doctrine. The more we become like Him, the more our actions, feelings, and efforts will never fail but will endure forever.

*I*t is not possible to come unto Christ

with all of our hearts if our hearts are tied in

knots with envy or anger or resentment or

pride. It's not possible to have a mighty

change of heart if we're harboring grudges.

It's not possible to give our hearts to God

when they're laden with the baggage of sin

or regret or spiritual neglect. And yet, all the

Lord really wants from us is our hearts.

We are the followers of Jesus Christ. And we have been His followers and have loved Him for a long, long time. Nothing is more important than working and sacrificing and enduring for Him.

The Lord has set no limits on what He is willing to teach us and give us. We are the only ones who set limits—through our neglect or disobedience or ignorance. We are in large measure the ones who determine what we will learn and experience in mortality, and what we will receive eternally.

If you want to know the Lord,

go to work for Him.

SIN MAKES US STUPID, AND IT COSTS A LOT TOO—A LOT OF

TIME, MONEY, PEACE OF MIND, OPPORTUNITY TO PROGRESS,

SELF-RESPECT, INTEGRITY, VIRTUE, AND THE TRUST OF LOVED

ONES. SO REPENT NOW. REPENT DAILY. FOR THOSE WHO

WANT TO BE SANCTIFIED, REPENTANCE IS NOT OPTIONAL.

With the exception of those serving full-time missions, we needn't don name badges or knock on doors to help build the kingdom. For though some would portray us as dowdy and dominated rather than the dynamic, radiant women we are, no woman is more persuasive, no woman has greater influence for good, no woman is a more vibrant instrument in the hands of the Lord than a woman of God who is thrilled to be who she is. I like to think of us as the Lord's secret weapon. If we did have name tags, I would want mine to read: "Sheri Dew, Woman of God, Busy Building the Kingdom of God."

Ultimately we will become what we give our hearts to, for we are shaped by what we desire and seek after. If we love the Lord such that our hearts are changed, His image will fill our countenances. But if we love the world more, we'll slowly take upon us those characteristics.

When we label one another, we make judgments that divide us from each other and inevitably alienate us from the Lord. . . . We gain nothing by segregating ourselves based on superficial differences. What we have in common—particularly our commitment to the same glorious cause—is so much more significant than any distinctions in our individual lives.

The best way I know to strengthen our personal testimonies and protect ourselves from evil is to seek to have as many experiences with the Lord as possible. Regular immersion in the scriptures is one way to have regular experiences with the Lord. The scriptures are a conduit for revelation. They teach us the language of the Spirit, the language of revelation.

If sixty-second ads can influence us to spend money we don't have to buy things we don't need to impress people we don't even like, then how will minutes, hours, months, and years of watching infidelity, violence, and promiscuity affect us? The litmus test for entertainment of any kind is simple: Can you watch or participate in it and still have the Spirit with you?

From the beginning, Satan has sought to confuse us about our stewardships and distinctive natures as men and women. He has bombarded us with bizarre messages about gender, marriage, family, and all male-female relationships. He would have us believe men and women are so alike that our unique gifts are not necessary, or are so different that we can never hope to understand each other. Neither message is true. Our Father knew exactly what He was doing when He created us. He made us enough alike to love each other, but enough different that we would need to unite our strengths and stewardships to create a whole. Neither man nor woman is complete without the other.

*J*esus Christ is not our last chance, He

is our only chance. He will show us the

way because He is the way.

$\mathscr{T}$he word that best describes

leadership by a woman is *mother*.

And by a man is *father*.

We believe in progression, and progression is by design difficult. Though our knees buckle at times under life's pressures, none of us want to stay just like we are. Embedded within our spirits is the need to become more and more like our Father.

Within the priesthood is the power to separate and safeguard us from the world; the power to subdue the adversary and surmount obstacles; the power to comfort, bless, heal, and inoculate the righteous against the forces of darkness; the power to enlarge our capacity and enable us to hear the voice of the Lord; the power to strengthen marriages and families and bind us to each other; and the power to triumph over mortality and come unto Him. These blessings may be received by every righteous, seeking son or daughter of God.

The most effective way to share the gospel is to live it. When we live like disciples of Christ should live, when we aren't just good but happy to be good, others will be drawn to us.

The object of this life is not to become perfect.

That comes later. The object of mortality is to

become increasingly pure. Purity is key to drawing

upon the power of the Lord. Purity is always a

characteristic of a true follower of Jesus Christ.

*T*he kind of power operating in our lives is entirely up to us. If God wants a powerful people who can withstand the wiles of the devil (and He does), and if we were born to lead in these latter days (and we were), then we need to understand how God makes His power available to us, and how we gain access to that power.

The two greatest women, the two greatest

heroines, of all time are the two women upon

whom the entire plan of salvation depended:

Eve, whose choice in Eden initiated the Fall,

and Mary, who was worthy and willing to

bear the mortal Messiah. Both were firsts,

elected to go where no woman had gone before.

119

We must each walk through life on our own, but we don't have to do it alone. God wants a powerful people. He gives His power to those who are faithful. We have a sacred obligation to seek after the power of God and then to use that power as He directs. And when we have the power of God with us, nothing is impossible.

*I*f we could comprehend how majestic and glorious a righteous woman made perfect in the celestial kingdom will be, we would rise up and never be the same again. We would gladly take upon us the name of Christ—which means following Him, becoming like Him, and dedicating ourselves to Him and His work. Women of God who honor their covenants look differently, dress differently, respond to crises differently, and act and speak differently from women who have not made the same covenants. Women of God who know who they are have influence that has no limit and no end.

Why do we compete with each other? If we were all working at our peak every day to build the kingdom, which none of us are capable of doing, there would still be more to do. Why do we make comparisons that are never fair? Why do we sometimes label others when no one can be defined by a one-dimensional category. We're not supposed to be alike. We have different gifts. The Lord needs a full spectrum of talent consecrated to His work—which is why comparing, competing, and categorizing are deadly.

Read D&C 138 and Abraham 3 about the noble and great ones,

and ask the Lord if those verses have anything to do with you.

Ask Him to talk to you, through the Spirit, about you. When

you understand, without equivocation, that you were chosen

and reserved for now, and when you live in harmony with that

mission and with the promises you made premortally, you'll be

happier than you have ever been before. That is a promise.

*H*ere are a few questions to consider as we study and ponder the word of God: Do we understand that when we leave the temple we emerge armed with power, what kind of power it is, and how we gain access to that power? Do we know that the power of Jesus Christ is greater than any power Satan can muster? Have we experienced for ourselves that the Atonement can heal our broken hearts, can help us turn our mortal weakness into strength? Do we understand why sexual purity is so important to the Lord, and why He feels so strongly about marriage and the family?

We are the only ones who can show our young women and young men that it is possible to live with purity in a polluted world. We are the only ones who can show them that purity is not prudish and that vulgarity is not in vogue. And we are the only ones who can show them that a woman who has the Spirit with her is radiant, and a man of God who honors the priesthood he holds is the finest example of manhood to be found.

Neither Adam with his priesthood nor Eve with her motherhood could bring about the Fall alone. Their unique roles were interconnected. They counseled with and consoled one another, learned and grew together, lifted burdens neither could have lifted alone, and then faced the wilderness, with all of its uncertainty, together. This is the Lord's pattern for righteous men and women.

Some will try to persuade us as sisters that because we are not ordained to the priesthood, we have been shortchanged. These individuals are simply wrong and do not understand the gospel of Jesus Christ. The blessings of the priesthood are available to every righteous man and woman. We may all receive the Holy Ghost, obtain personal revelation, and be endowed in the temple, from which we emerge armed with power.

If you're serious about sanctification,

you can expect to experience heart-

wrenching moments that try your faith,

your endurance, and your patience.

While life is meant to test, challenge, and strengthen us, if we are attempting to negotiate the twists and turns and ups and downs of mortality alone, we're doing it all wrong. Mortality is a test, but it is an open-book test. We have access not only to the divine text but to Him who authored it.

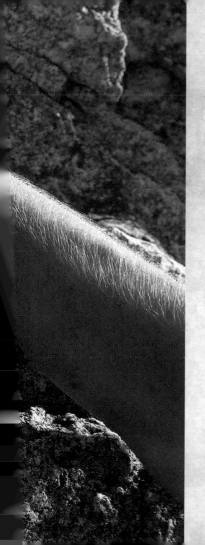

*I*f you won't listen to and learn from

others, the best you can do is the best

YOU can do.

*H*ere is the truth about womanhood. Our Father gave His daughters a divine endowment of gifts that give us unique influence. First and foremost, we have the high privilege of bearing children. If mortality is the time in all eternity to prove ourselves, then there is nothing more important than bearing children and leading them along the path home. Our Father also gifted us with the nature to nurture, keen sensitivity to the Spirit, selflessness, discernment, and heroic faith. No wonder our Father placed us at the heart of the family and thus at the center of the plan of salvation.

*I*n the temple we learn what it means to

be "in but not of" the world. We learn how to

live a higher law, even a terrestrial or celestial

law, while still residing in a telestial sphere.

$\mathcal{F}$aith is a principle of action. It is our willingness to believe in the

Savior that unleashes His power in our lives. Faith is not a bulwark

against tribulation, but an assurance that the Lord is overseeing all.

Is it possible that in this twilight season of the dispensation of the fulness of times, that we who have been armed with the most potent antidote on earth—the gift of the Holy Ghost—don't fully partake of that gift? Are we guilty of spiritually just "getting by" and not accessing the power and protection within our reach? Are we satisfied with far less than the Lord is willing to give us, essentially opting to go it alone here rather than partner with the Divine?

Imagine what would happen in this Church if every morning six million of us got on our knees and asked our Father who He needed us to reach out to that day. And then imagine if we did it! Imagine if we consecrated our energy and focused en masse to the greatest service of all—leading our brothers and sisters to Christ. Imagine what will happen when we mobilize the sisters of Relief Society to stand together to help build the kingdom. We will see the awakening and arising of a sleeping, slouching giant. I invite you to stand tall, to thrust in your sickle and join in this work with vigor. I invite you to rededicate your life to building the kingdom. To reach out to someone. To make a difference in someone's life spiritually. None of us have to reach everyone. But what if we all reached someone?

I have not been able to identify any organization anywhere in the world where women have more influence than in this Church. There is no group of women anywhere who teach more, lead more, or speak more—or are better at it. Right now, hundreds of thousands of us are teaching children, youth, and adults. Hundreds of thousands more enjoy the rights and responsibilities of presidency. Where else do women bear such weighty responsibility and enjoy such influence? And there is no other organization for women that rivals the Relief Society, which is the most important gathering of women on this side of the veil. Therefore, we are the ones who need to define Latter-day Saint womanhood, not anyone else. This means speaking up and reaching out. It means seeking to have influence with as many people as possible.

As mothers in Israel, our influence comes from a divine endowment that has been in place from the beginning. In the premortal world, when our Father described our role, I wonder if we didn't stand in wide-eyed wonder that He would bless us with a sacred trust so central to His plan and that He would endow us with gifts so vital to the loving and leading of His children. I wonder if we shouted for joy at least in part because of the ennobling stature He gave us in His kingdom.

LIFE IS A TEST. IT IS ONLY A TEST—MEANING, THAT'S ALL IT IS. NOTHING MORE, BUT NOTHING LESS. IT IS A TEST OF OUR CONVICTIONS AND PRIORITIES, OUR FAITH AND FAITHFULNESS, OUR PATIENCE AND RESILIENCE, AND IN THE END, OUR ULTIMATE DESIRES. IT IS A TEST TO DETERMINE IF WE WANT TO BE PART OF THE KINGDOM OF GOD MORE THAN WE WANT ANYTHING ELSE.

Some of the photos in this book have particular meaning to the author, as follows: